MASSIMO WOLKE

Cock
Unicorns
COLORING BOOK

MASSIMO WOLKE

Cock
Unicorns
COLORING BOOK

Bibliografische Information der Deutschen Nationalbibliothek:
Die Deutsche Nationalbibliothek verzeichnet diese Publikation in der
Deutschen Nationalbibliografie; detaillierte bibliografische Daten sind im
Internet über http://dnb.dnb.de abrufbar.

© 2022 Massimo Wolke
2. Auflage
Herstellung und Verlag:
BoD - Books on Demand, Norderstedt

ISBN: 978-3-7494-2089-6

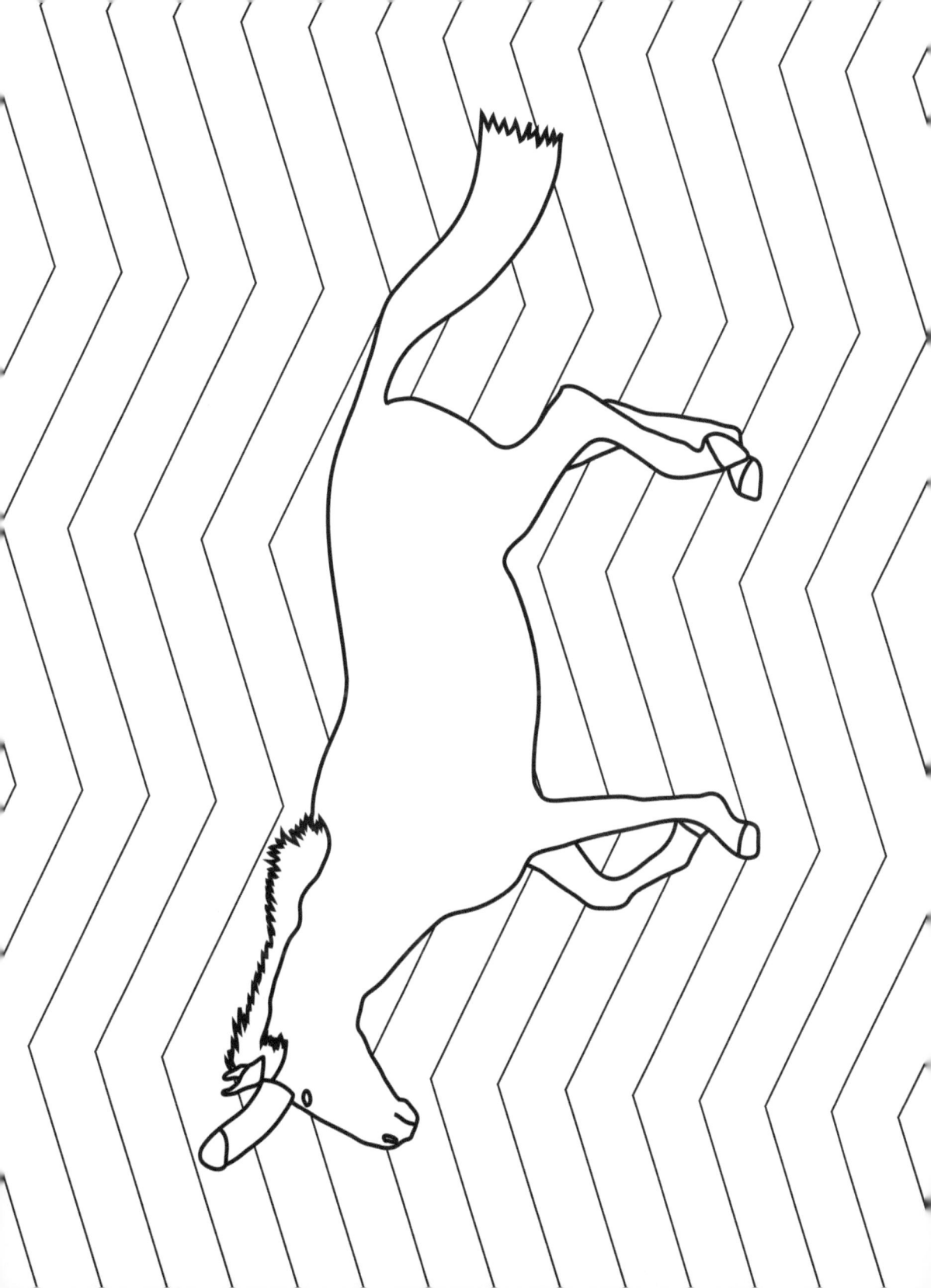

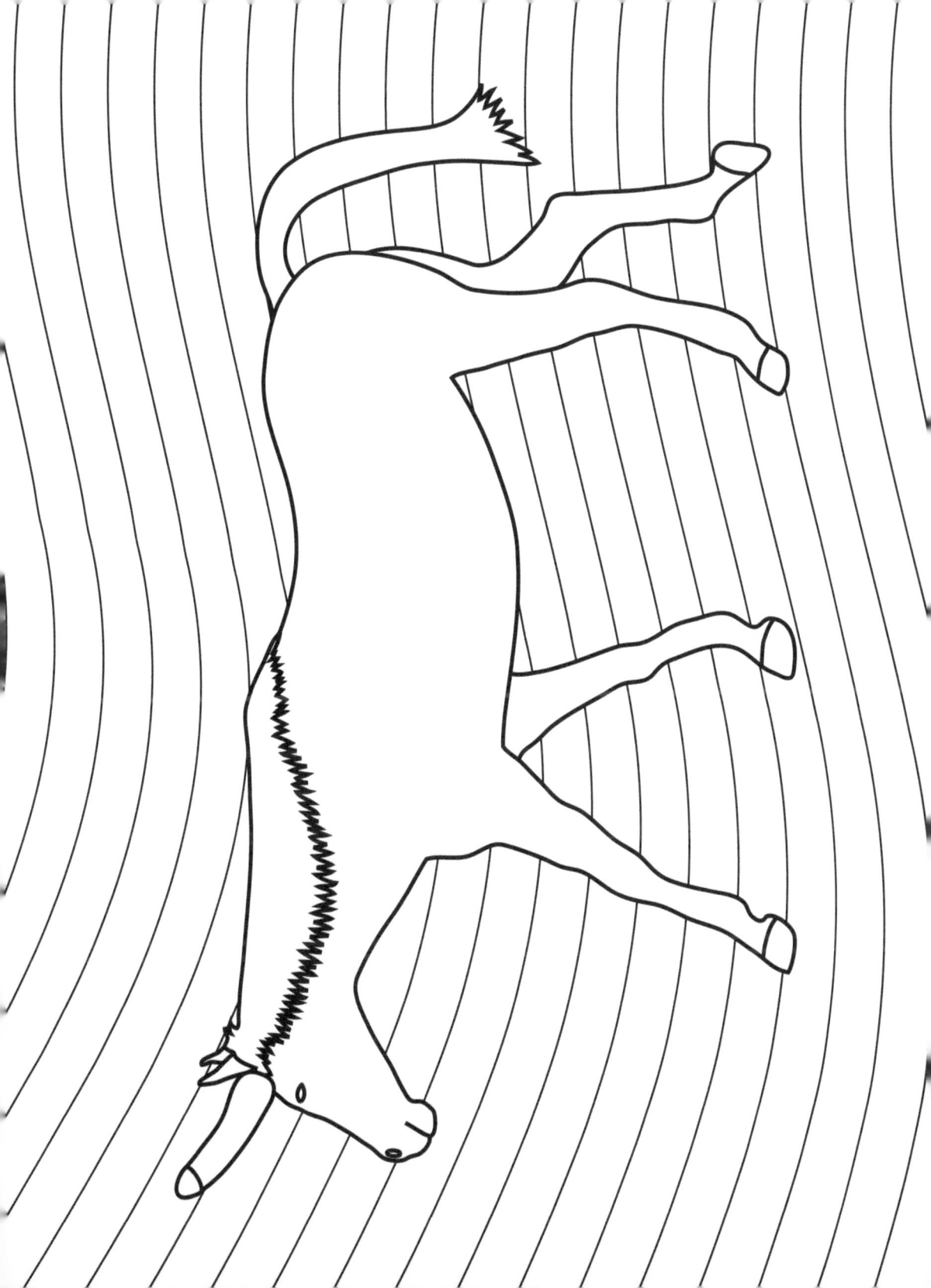

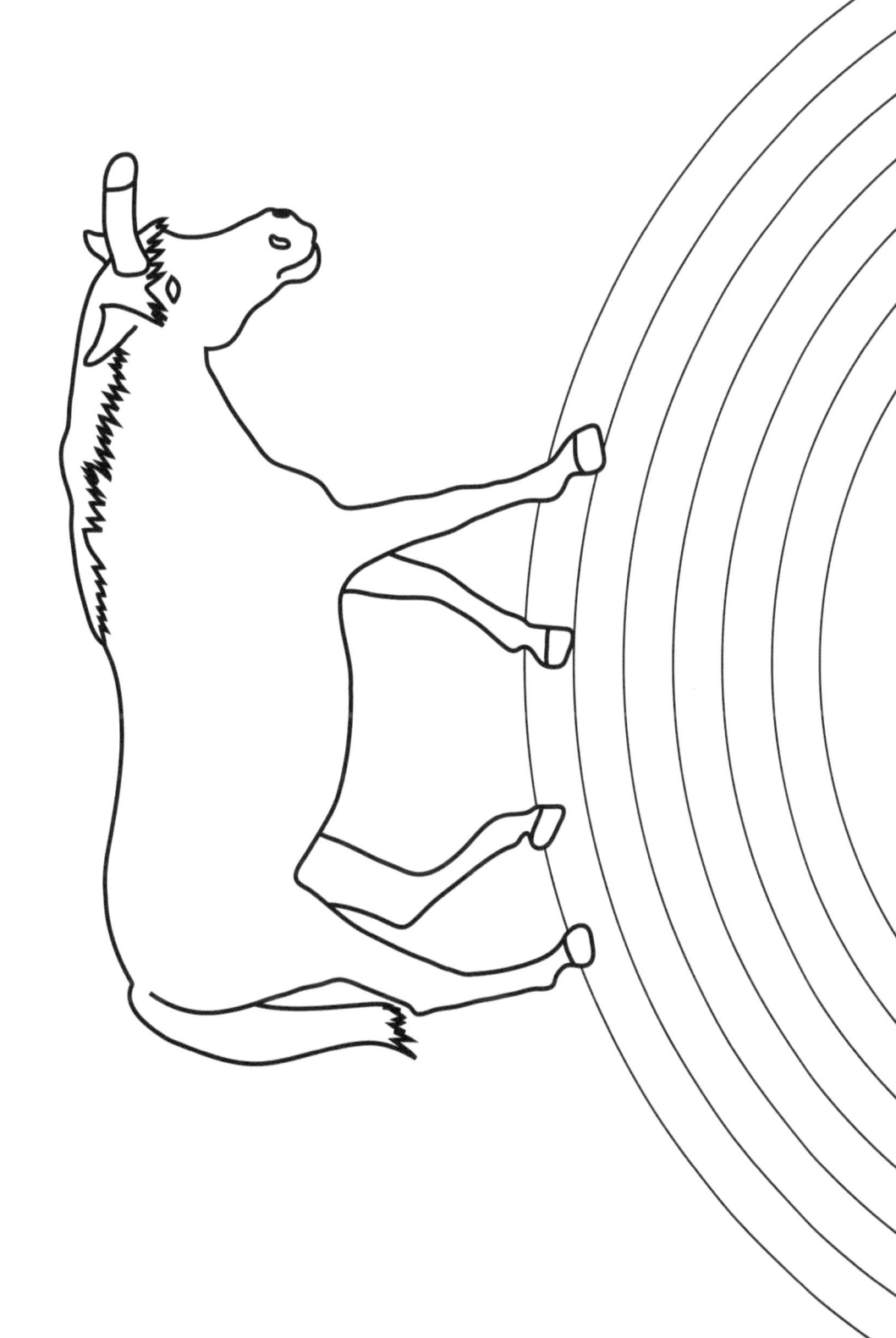

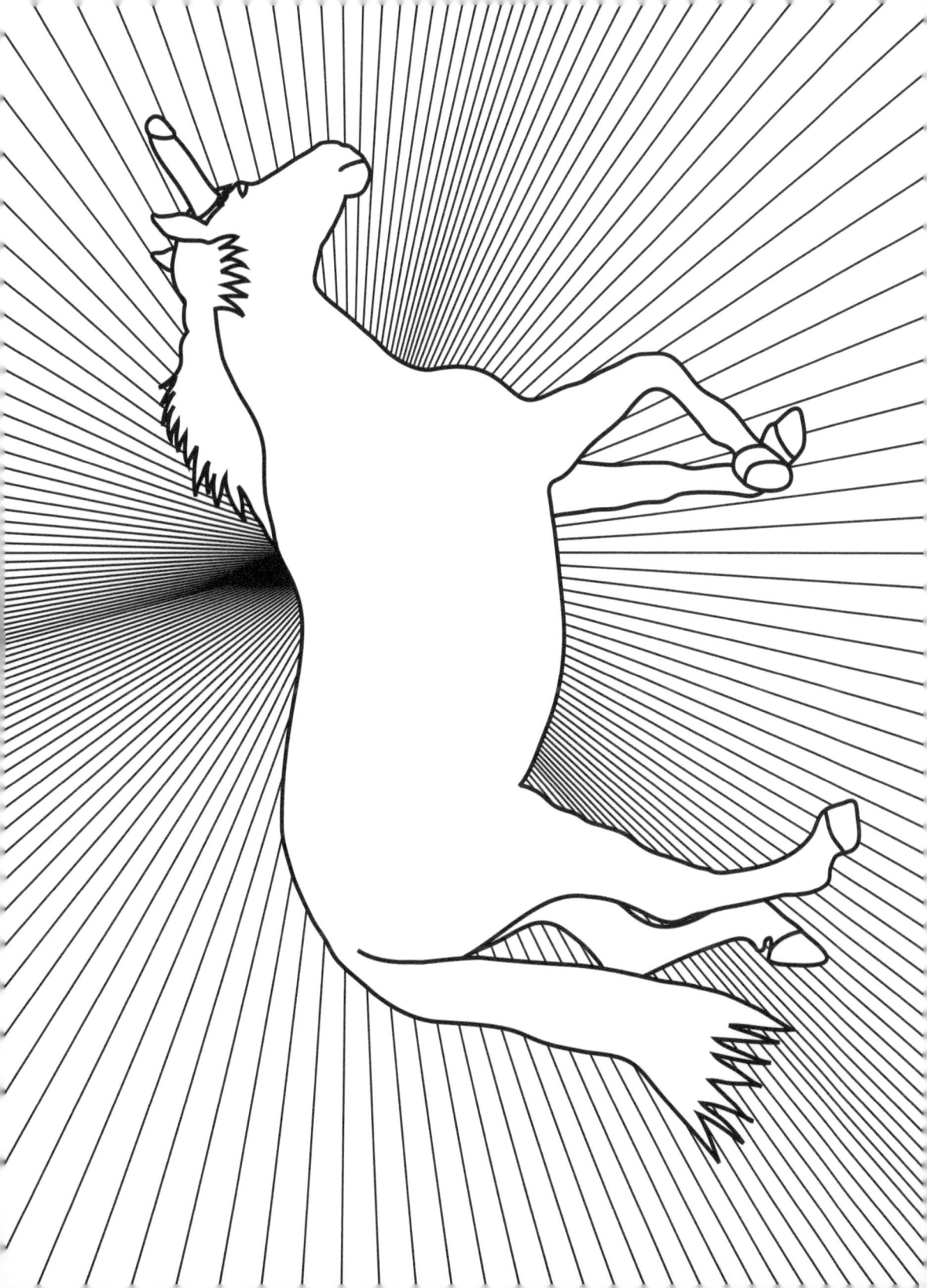